iDisciple

STEP BY STEP
GEN Z CURRICULUM
FOR CHURCH LEADERS

JODY G. TADROS

WESTBOW
PRESS®
A DIVISION OF THOMAS NELSON
& ZONDERVAN

This book is a work of non-fiction. Unless otherwise noted, the author
and the publisher make no explicit guarantees as to the accuracy of
the information contained in this book and in some cases, names
of people and places have been altered to protect their privacy.

WestBow Press books may be ordered through
booksellers or by contacting:

WestBow Press
A Division of Thomas Nelson & Zondervan
1663 Liberty Drive
Bloomington, IN 47403
www.westbowpress.com
844-714-3454

Scripture quotations are from New Revised Standard Version Bible,
copyright © 1989 National Council of the Churches of Christ in the United
States of America. Used by permission. All rights reserved worldwide.

ISBN: 978-1-6642-1493-4 (sc)
ISBN: 978-1-6642-1495-8 (hc)
ISBN: 978-1-6642-1494-1 (e)

Library of Congress Control Number: 2020923912

Print information available on the last page.

WestBow Press rev. date: 12/16/2020

In memory of Pastor Adham Farid,
my mentor and friend who taught me
how to be and make disciples.

Contents

Foreword

Jody Tadros emphasizes Christian discipleship, and he specifically emphasizes the importance of discipleship training for young people who are part of Generation Z. There are many ways, of course, to characterize different generations: Baby Boomers, Generation X (Busters), Generation Y (Millennials), and now Generation Z. Experts have tried to characterize Generation Z (or Gen Z), consisting of children born between 1995 and 2012. They have been called the "iGeneration" or "Selfie Generation." Yet, their particular characteristics, values, and goals are unique. Christians should be attentive to these particularities if they want to minister effectively to Gen Z.

Tadros utilizes biblical teaching about Christian discipleship along with contemporary literature on the topic. For example, he uses literature from the Navigators, and adapts their methodology specifically for the sake of discipling Gen Z young people. Tadros emphasizes the importance of time concerns characteristic of Gen Z. They are technologically savvy, and they expect quick and internet sophisticated communication. In other words, they need to be treated as *iDisciples*, as Tadros's title suggests. Churches cannot expect that longstanding practices for discipleship training will work with young people who are expert in video games, Facebook, Instagram, and Snapchat. Leaders in discipleship, of course, must adapt empathetically as well as creatively to each new generation.

Church leaders also need to develop trust with Gen Z young people. Although their technological skills are sophisticated and most likely surpass the skills of their mentors, they are still human beings with the same spiritual and relational needs as others. It's not easy to earn the trust of young people of any generation. However, awareness of the unique characteristics of Gen Z will help, coupled with the willingness to adapt to their favored methods of communication, including social media.

In a post coronavirus pandemic world, Christians in general and church leaders in particular must realize that ministry cannot rely on "business as usual," so to speak, in ministering today. They must be responsive to the demanding needs of people and of society, and provide opportunities for ministry that they probably never imagined. For example: Live streaming worship services? Sermon, devotional, and teaching videos? Online small groups? Zoom youth gatherings? FaceTime mentoring? Who knows what Christians may need to do in ministering today to people, both inside and outside their churches? Perhaps in emphasizing discipleship for Gen Z, the young people to whom we're ministering will in turn help us minister better by utilizing their technological know-how as *iDisciples*!

Dr. Don Thorsen, Ph.D. A published author and professor at Azusa Pacific Seminary, Department of Biblical and Theological Studies.

Preface

At the beginning of my seminary, the idea of authoring a book started to grow in my mind that I was thinking about it day and night for two years. Even though I knew the topic, I did not know how to execute it and I started to give up. A couple of years past by, during one of my theology classes, Dr. Don Thorsen challenged my peers and I to author a book. He took the first day of class explaining the various parts on how to create a non-fiction. During that time, the Holy Spirit stirred my heart again. My desire was reborn to author a book about the importance of discipleship in the church for generations to come. It was the start of long years of research on how to write a book on the topic of discipleship.

Throughout my seminary classes, I had the privilege to study the different views on discipleship from great theologians and philosophers, such as USC professor Dallas Willard, the various writings of Dietrich Bonhoeffer, and other notable authors. By the time I reached my capstone class to write my thesis, I had compiled many ideas and views, helping me to develop a program tailored to the coming generation, generation Z.

After all these years of researching and collecting the different ideas about discipleship, I am still learning new ideas on how to tackle the problems of discipleship in the church. I believe that discipleship is vital to the church and in advancing the kingdom. The methodology will always go through many transformations, adapting it to each generation.

This book provides a methodology in helping pastors and laypeople of any church congregations to assist mentors to develop the coming generation, Gen Z. It is my prayers that the information in this book will help churches embrace the importance of discipleship by obeying the command of our Lord Jesus Chris to "GO and Make Disciples!"

Acknowledgment

Writing a book is not an easy project. It takes mental dedication and encouragements to keep going, especially during the times you just want to quit. First, I want to thank my wife and best friend, Manar for her encouragements and support during the process. I want to thank my family for their support through my seminary studies.

Second, I want to thank Azusa Pacific Seminary's faculty and staff for giving me the tools and understanding during my seminary experience to put together what I learned into this book project: Rob Muthiah, Brian Lugioyo, Keith Matthews, and Kevin Young. Also, I want to thank Kent Walkemeyer for guiding me through my capstone thesis and helping me put the ideas in this book together. Don Thorsen for challenging his classes to author a book. Likewise, for taking time out of his busy schedule to read the manuscript and write the forward. Dr. Karen Winslow for making me fall in love with the Old Testament and guiding me with different resources and ideas while drafting my thesis. Finally, I want to thank the writing center for helping me polish my final draft and for guiding me through the process.

Third, I want to thank Valerie Morcos for opening her home and taking the time out of her busy schedule to edit my thesis all the way until submission day. I also want to thank the Sanctuary church for their support through prayers and encouragements: Pastor Marty Walker, Jonathan & Dawn Edwards, Jen Lord and Rachel Edwards.

Fourth, I want to thank my friends, Pastor Tyler Delphous, former Junior & High School pastor at the Sanctuary, for helping me collect students research data. Also, Pastor Brandon Maddux, former children ministries at the Sanctuary for praying for me during this project and taking the time to listen and perfect my ideas about discipleship.

Last but not least, a special appreciation to the Baker family for opening their home and making my wife and I feel that we are part of the church family. I want to thank David Baker for taking the time to read and edit my thesis out of his busy travel schedule and guiding me through the process. Also, I would love to thank author and speaker Toria Leigh for helping with the ideas on how to publish my book. Moreover, I want to thank Westbow Press for guiding me through the publishing process.

Finally, I want to give a big thanks, honor and glory to my God and savior Jesus Christ for giving me the strength physically, mentally, and emotionally while writing my thesis and putting this book project together.

PART 1

The Narrative and The Problem

Go therefore and make disciples of all nations,
baptizing them in the name of the Father
and of the Son and of the Holy Spirit, [20]and
teaching them to obey everything that I
have commanded you. And remember, I am
with you always, to the end of the age.
—Matthew 28:19-20 (NRSV)

Introduction

On an episode of *The Ellen DeGeneres Show*, Ellen invites a young woman from the audience to play a game. Ellen tells this young woman that she needs to read an actual physical map for directions, she needs to look up a phone number of a specific business inside the yellow pages, and finally dial the number using an old, antique rotary cordless phone. All that under a limited given time. This woman could not read the map, could not find the number without Ellen's help, and at first did not know how to use the antique phone. As I watched this episode my mind took me to the coming generation, Gen Z, and all the technology that boomed in the last few years, which changed the view of society when it comes to politics, education, economy, values, ethics, and morals. Furthermore, I began to think about how technology will impact the church, specifically, the implementation of making disciples for the kingdom of God.

Jesus' last command to his disciples was to go and make disciples of all nations. Although the foundation and principles of biblical discipleship from biblical times until the present remain the same, by necessity the methodology and its implementation must adapt for each generation accordingly. This need for adapting has never been truer than it is now for generation Z. True biblical discipleship is a command that the church has increasingly neglected throughout the generations, especially in our twenty first century. In my own life, being a disciple under my mentor was a significant tool that God used to develop me into the person I am today. It made me realize the crucial importance of discipleship.

My Story

In February of 2001, I surrendered my life to Christ at a youth camp in Vista, San Diego. After my conversion, I did not know what the next step was in following Jesus especially coming from the Orthodox faith. I had many questions that I needed answers for, but sadly, my church leaders did not give me any answers to my questions, but rather they made me more confused and told me that I needed to earn my way to heaven and that salvation was not by grace. After a couple of weeks, my camp leaders called me and asked me if I would be interested in getting together with someone to mentor me and explain in depth what it means to follow Jesus. Without hesitation, I said yes, and I began my journey with my mentor.

I recall my first meeting with my mentor. It was not with my cabin leaders; rather it was with the senior pastor, Pastor Adham Farid, who oversaw the camp. I met him at his church in a room that looked like the attic of a church building. It did not have air conditioning, and there was only a small fan that blew out hot air. As I entered the room, there was a small table and two chairs. He sat in one of the chairs and I sat on the other. On the table there was a binder with "Making Disciples" written on it. When I sat down across from him, we began to talk about my life, how I came to the United States of America, and about accepting Jesus as my savior.

After I finished talking about my background and experience, my mentor began to explain what we would be doing during our times together. He began to set rules that both of us needed to abide by to make this time together beneficial. The rules were: (1) we will meet every Thursday for one hour, (2) read the lesson and memorize the scripture of the day from the "Making Disciples" binder, and (3) be able to disciple another person after I finish the program. I was excited and terrified at the same time because I realized that there was no one else joining me on this journey. It was on this very day that my life with Christ took another step forward: I became a disciple.

During my appointments with Pastor Adham many questions started to arise and talking about them deepened our relationship together. After several meetings, I started to attend his youth ministry every Thursday night. He encouraged me to start leading worship for the youth and taught me how to hear the voice of the Holy Spirit during services to let Him lead through me. Our times together were not just studying the word of God; but rather many times he took me fishing with him and his family, which taught me patience in my own life. As I faced problems at home, school, and work, he brought me back to the word of God and taught me how to pray. He taught me how to be direct with people and that my answers needed to be either "Yes" or "No" without "buts". When I needed correction, he was firm yet loving at the same time. He did not yell at me but would gently explain his point of view by tying it back to the word of God. As I got deeper in the Bible, he pushed me to take my first sermon during the Christmas service for the youth. He believed in me when I did not believe in myself. As I grew in my faith with Christ, he started taking me to the yearly youth camps, the place of my conversion, and I became a cabin leader for the coming generation. It was during one of these camps that he had a heart attack and went to be with the Lord. It was very hard for me to accept his loss because I saw his life's impact on my own generation. His life's legacy deeply influenced my life and so many others. It led me to understand and comprehend the importance of making disciples. God never intended the church to be alone in this journey called life. It was because of my mentor that I decided to enter seminary and continue his legacy for generations to come.

The Problem

As I started serving in different churches, within the youth ministry context, I began to observe that being a disciple was just an option in many churches that I attended. The importance of discipleship was not on the radar of the church. There were not any teachings on the significance of being a disciple, especially for those who just gave their lives to Jesus Christ. I started to investigate the reasons behind the church's lack of having mentors to disciple the young generation on their newfound faith. One of the reasons I came across was the aspect of time. When I talked to church leaders and youth pastors, they pulled out the time card as a big contributor to the reason why the church lacks programs and teachings on discipleship. Growing up in this fast-paced media world, mentors and disciples do not have time to spend together to discuss and share life together. Mentors were not willing to take the time and do the hard work of walking alongside each person to rebuke, encourage, and discipline in order to be used by the Holy Spirit to transform each person into the image of Jesus Christ.

The second reason that I discovered was the issue of trust between mentors and mentees. Believers are afraid to trust mentors with their lives due to past hurts and bad experiences. When I talked to youths, I always got the same responses, "I don't have anyone I can trust," or "Why do I need someone to tell me what to do in my life?" It was sad to see a generation that sorely lacked in mentors and discipleship.

This issue of trust as well as the issue of limited time in the busy modern world are the two main obstacles that have hindered discipleship. These factors are the direct result of the increased absence of teachings on discipleship in the church. By increasingly succumbing to the distractions of life, the church has slowly moved away from a focus on this central command of Jesus Christ to His followers. Not being proactive and addressing these issues has clearly failed.

I conclude that the main cause for not making disciples in the church is due to lack of knowledge and misunderstanding of what true discipleship is according to the Bible. If church leaders truly understood the importance and centrality of Jesus' command, they would desire to be equipped to teach on and implement the principles of discipleship. As I came to an understanding of what has worked and what has not worked for successful discipleship, I decided to write about the misconceptions of discipleship and educate this generation, generation Z, on true discipleship.

For this reason, this book is on the importance

of understanding discipleship from a biblical point of view, through developing and implementing the Navigators' 2:7 series discipleship program. It is a curriculum for churches targeting today's generation of youth. The Navigators is a worldwide discipleship ministry out of Colorado Springs, Colorado. Its focus is on discipling Christians with the emphasis on sharing the gospel and their faith with others in their communities through life-to-life relationships. Their mission statement is, "To know Christ, make him known, and help others do the same." The curriculum is just a tool for pastors and church leaders to develop the necessary mentor and mentee relationships for making disciples.

I believe that this generation is in need of people who can come alongside them to show them how to live and be image-bearers and imitators of Jesus Christ in a dark and depraved world. I believe that the church needs to step up to the plate and have a global vision of discipleship rather than playing church and being afraid of the surrounding culture. I believe that discipleship is not a program put together by the church to make people religious, but rather it is relational. It is how a community hears the call of discipleship coming straight from Jesus himself, becoming a life journey of transforming disciples into the image of Christ.

The Solution

Therefore, I propose to develop a comprehensive discipleship process for youth built upon the Navigators' discipleship system and emphasizing one-on-one discipleship relationships. This book curriculum will offer training to pastors, youth pastors, and other youth leaders to equip them for this discipleship process.

PART 2

Biblical & Theological Foundation

Examples of Disciples and Discipleship in the Old and New Testaments

Introduction

To be able to have a comprehensive mentor and mentee relationship for generation Z and coming generations, one needs to go back and ask the question, what is discipleship? Is it biblical? Moreover, how can a person be a disciple of Jesus? Does one have a choice, or is it a matter of obedience? Many people believe they can live without having another person constantly involved in their lives, whether they are correcting them to help them reach their best or encouraging them when they are going through hard times. I believe many believers are not growing into God's potential for them because they are missing this crucial concept of discipleship in their lives. In Dietrich Bonhoeffer, "The Cost of Discipleship", he says, "Jesus' commandment never wishes to destroy life, but rather to preserve, strengthen, and heal life."[1] Many believers think that discipleship would be a burden on them, rather than what it actually does which is freeing them from all rules and legalism.

---

[1] Clifford J. Green and Michael P. DeJonge, eds., *The Bonhoeffer Reader* (Minneapolis: Fortress Press, 2013), 458.

Is Discipleship Biblical?

Before talking about what believers think regarding discipleship, we need to answer the question: Is it biblical? To answer this crucial question, we need to go back in time and examine examples from the biblical text.

Old Testament Examples

King David & The Prophet Samuel

First, I will examine the Old Testament. The first example is in the book of 1 Samuel. It is the story of King David and the prophet Samuel. The story is about David, a shepherd boy, tending his father's sheep. After the prophet Samuel anoints him the coming king over Jerusalem, King Saul attempts many times to kill David, but he misses, sending him to run away into exile to live in the mountains and near cities. Throughout his exile, David goes to the prophet Samuel when he encounters problems he does not know how to handle. The biblical text records in 1 Samuel 19, "Now David fled and escaped; he came to Samuel at Ramah and told him all that Saul had done to him. He and Samuel went and settled at Naioth." David goes to Samuel, the person who anointed him as king, to seek help, advice and refuge. The relational bond between David and the prophet Samuel is a key example in presenting the characteristics of discipleship for pastors and leaders in mentoring Generation Z. This relational bond gave

King David an open door to be able always go to Samuel for advice in time of need. Pastors and leaders need to have this relational understanding when it comes to discipleship for it opens the door for the coming generation to come to them openly and freely without feeling judged.

Moses & Joshua

Another example in the Old Testament is in the book of Numbers, the story of Moses and his right-hand military commander Joshua. As God calls Moses for the enormous task to lead the people of Israel out of Egypt, He was preparing Joshua through Moses' leadership to take the lead after him. Throughout the challenges of the journey in the wilderness, Joshua learns everything through Moses' obedience to God. In one incident, Moses sends twelve spies to spy on the land that the Lord tells them to take over and to bring a report. After scouting the land, Joshua and Caleb are the only two people, out of the twelve spies, who believe they should conquer the land flowing with milk and honey. In Numbers 14, it records that,

> Joshua son of Nun and Caleb son of Jephunneh, who were among those who had spied out the land, tore their clothes and said to all the congregation of the Israelites, "The land that we went

through as spies is an exceedingly good land. If the Lord is pleased with us, he will bring us into this land and give it to us, a land that flows with milk and honey. Only, do not rebel against the Lord; and do not fear the people of the land, for they are no more than bread for us; their protection is removed from them, and the Lord is with us; do not fear them." But the whole congregation threatened to stone them. Numbers 14:6-10

Joshua stands out in this situation as one who has great faith. Unlike most of his peers, his trust in God and his desire to obey Him is stronger than any fear. One needs to ask the question; from where did Joshua get his faith? Why was he not afraid like the others? It is because he had surrounded himself with Moses' influence. Moses' life of obedience to God stirs and builds Joshua's faith in his God. His actions speak louder than his words, teaching Joshua how to believe, trust, and have faith. The everyday actions taught Joshua how to lead Israel after Moses' death. For that reason God calls and appoints Joshua to be his successor to lead the people over to the promised land. In Numbers 27 the Lord says to Moses,

Take Joshua son of Nun, a man in whom is the spirit, and lay your hand upon him; have him stand before Eleazar the priest and all the congregation, and commission him in their sight. You shall give him some of your authority, so that all the congregation of the Israelites may obey. —Numbers 27: 18-20

Here we see that God acknowledges Joshua's obedience to God through his submission to Moses and entrusts him with the task of being the leader over Israel. Moses displays what mentees need to observe in their leaders when it comes to passing the baton to the next generation. Youth directors always need to have their eyes open on the next generation, setting their lives as an example to follow them according to the values and ethics of a biblical worldview. The obedient life of Moses toward YAHWE showed Joshua the truth about his God and developed in him an obedient heart that promoted him from a soldier to a leader. It is the leader's responsibility in the church to show the next generation how to follow Christ through the relational process of discipleship.

Through these two stories, one can see that disciple-making is important throughout the Old Testament text. Wilkins notes, "Even though the terms for disciple are not found in abundance in the Old Testament, various relationships in Israel were true 'discipleship' relations since they share universal characteristics of discipleship relations."[2] Wilkens

[2] Michael J. Wilkins, *Following the Master: A Biblical Theology of Discipleship* (Grand Rapids: Zondervan Publishing, 1992), 52.

points out the somewhat hidden discipleship theme throughout the Old Testament scriptures. One story after another exhibits some characteristic of disciple making.

New Testament Examples

Paul & Timothy

In addition, the New Testament shares other stories that illustrate the importance of discipleship in the life of the believer. The first narrative that I will observe is the relationship between Paul and his young disciple Timothy. Timothy is one of the people who was with Paul on his missionary journey. However, Paul did not want Timothy to continue with him because he was slowing him down throughout the trip. In the end, Paul imparts his wisdom and knowledge to young Timothy, making him the pastor at the church of Ephesus. Accordingly, he encourages him in his letters, "I am giving you these instructions, Timothy, my child, in accordance with the prophecies made earlier about you, so that by following them you may fight the good fight, having faith and a good conscience." (1 Timothy 1:18-19). He continues encouraging Timothy and building his self-esteem and confidence for being a young pastor among an older congregation, "Let no one despise your youth, but set the believers an example in speech and conduct, in love, in faith, in purity." (1 Timothy 4:12). Timothy is to set an example to the Ephesian believers as Paul set a model for him to imitate. In *The Complete Book of Discipleship*, Bill Hull explains that, "experiencing the Christlike qualities of someone close to us provides a powerful illustration of what God in person looks like. Paul believed so strongly in this principle that he believed Timothy's transformation demonstrated it."[3] Paul believes in Timothy so much that he sends him to the Corinthian church to be an imitator of Christ for them: "I appeal to you, then, be imitators of me. For this reason I sent you Timothy, who is my beloved and faithful child in the Lord, to remind you of my ways in Christ Jesus, as I teach them everywhere in every church." (1 Corinthians 4:16-17). According to Hull, "Timothy will remind people of Paul's way in Christ, which in turn will remind people of Christ."[4] The Biblical text highlights the importance of discipleship and being imitators to others as in the relationship between Paul and his son in the Lord Timothy.

Paul's encouragement to young Timothy is what Gen Z and the coming generations look for from the previous generations. The church needs to learn to speak the words of encouragement from the apostle Paul as a tool in discipling Gen Zers. In a world that is full of animosity and psychological abuse in the

---

[3] Bill Hull, *The Complete Book of Discipleship: On Being and Making Followers of Christ* (Colorado Springs: Navpress, 2006), 115.
[4] Hull, 115.

education and family systems, this generation is in need of hearing words of encouragement to uplift their soul and spirit in a dark and depraved world; if they cannot find it in the church where are they going to find it? Moreover, Paul believed in Timothy's abilities and gifts, looking beyond his inadequate low-self-esteem, and pushing him to rise up to the task of being a young pastor by lifting up his soul and spirit through his encouraging words. In order to disciple the coming generation, Pastors need to be a Paul for all the young Timothies in their communities through their words of encouragement and by stirring up the gifts inside each disciple.

Jesus Christ & The Disciples

Another example of discipleship in the New Testament is the account of Jesus Christ and the disciples. Through Jesus' paradigm of choosing disciples, He puts forth the essential processes and key tasks for the church in transforming believers into disciples. During Jesus' ministry, He demonstrates the steps and methodology of raising disciples. First, He calls the twelve to follow Him. Second, He lives among them for three years teaching, rebuking, encouraging, and sending them to carry the message of the Gospel to the entire world. Third, He always has his close group Peter, James, and John. It is through a relational methodology that Christ raises up followers. In "Discipleshift", Jim Putman and Bobby Harrington write,

> Jesus not only told us to make disciples but also gave us a model to follow in doing so. I believe that most Christians have divorced the teachings of Jesus from the methods of Jesus, and yet they expect the results of Jesus. I believe his methods are just as divine as his teachings. He showed us that the fundamental methodology in making disciples is relationships grounded in truth and love. Jesus is the greatest disciple maker in history and his way works. Discipleship is the emphasis. Relationships are the method. Jesus invited people into relationships with himself; he loved them and in the process showed them how to follow God. His primary method was life-on-life.[5]

Putman and Harrington reveal the importance of discipleship as central to Jesus' ministry as it needs to be central for the church. Jesus' call for discipleship is the same from generation to generation, but the method of relationship is different.

The disciple model of Jesus Christ is what needs

---

[5] Jim Putman, Bobby Harrington, and Robert E. Coleman, *DiscipleShift: Five Steps That Help Your Church to Make Disciples Who Make Disciples* (Grand Rapids: Zondervan, 2013), 33.

to characterize discipleship in the church for the Z generation. Jesus demonstrates to the church some characteristics pastors and leaders need to develop in discipling others, especially the Gen Zers. His discipleship model exemplifies the aspect of time and trust among the disciples. Jesus gave time to his disciples. He did life with them and through it all they trusted Him and in return, He entrusted them with the biggest mission on earth, to go and make disciples of all nations. He also called disciples to himself. He extended the grace of discipleship, believing in His disciples that they will take the mission of the Gospel to all the earth to expand the kingdom of His Father. The church needs to extend the same grace to Gen Z, and all who come into a relationship with the Creator. When the focus of the church waivers away from its true calling of making disciples, outspreading the grace of God to the world, then the church, pastoral staff and the congregation has stopped being the hands and feet of Jesus in a world in need of hearing the Gospel of hope, the good news, in a hopeless and dying world.

The Jewish Culture
& Disciple-making

To develop an even deeper understanding of Jesus' model of discipleship, one must examine the ancient Jewish culture from which He came and see just how radically He differed. In early Judaism, rabbis pick only the best of the best to learn under them. Hull comments, "The Pharisees' demanding discipleship system rewarded only the best and brightest and was the doorway to a wonderful religious career."[6] In first-century discipleship, the teacher of the law does not ask the student to come and follow; rather it is the student's decision to follow the master. The student asks the teacher but at the same time, the teacher has the authority to accept or refuse the request. Hull states,

> Young men could join a variety of schools, each led by a rabbi or a teacher. In some cases, students chose their

---

[6] Hull, 60.

teacher and, of course, teachers could accept or reject a student's application. If a young man hadn't achieved a certain academic and social status by the time of his bar mitzvah at age thirteen, he would instead choose a life of farming, fishing, carpentry, or the like.[7]

In his article about the Lessons of the Fathers, found in the Mishnah, Reinhard Neudecker writes that rabbis are to have as many disciples to impart wisdom and knowledge to until their old age; nevertheless, they are to pick only the best that excel in the oral and written traditions. In early Judaism, the importance of following a master is described by Neudecker. It states in the Mishnah in tractate (Av 1:6,16): "Produce for yourself a master."

> This call is addressed to every youth. The study of Torah under a master is of a higher priority than the commandment to honor one's parents; the injunction to practice loving acts of kindness and the duty to establish peace among people. Torah study is considered a form of the worship of God; it is the very purpose of one's existence.[8]

---

[7] Ibid., 63.

[8] Reinhard Neudecker, "Master-Disciple/Disciple-Master Relationship in Rabbinic Judaism and in the Gospels," *Gregorianum* 80, no. 2 (1999): 249.

As we can see disciple making was very important in the Jewish culture in early Judaism. Jesus did not abolish this disciple-making process, but rather radically transformed it. For Jesus' followers, being a disciple is still important and central to their existence, however he picked his disciples and did not just pick the well-educated but in fact a mix of people ranging from poor fishermen to despised tax collectors.

These differences often led to confusion on the part of the Jewish people. Michael Wilkins, New Testament professor of language and literature at Talbot School of Theology writes,

> Discipleship in the ancient world was a common phenomenon. It primarily involved commitment of an individual to a great master or leader. The kind of commitment varied with the type of master. The important feature for us to understand is that when Jesus came and called men and women to follow him, not all understood him in the same way.[9]

Jesus maintained the rabbinical relational process between the teacher and His students. His way was not a program for the masses, and also what caused some confusion was that His methods were not simply a transfer of knowledge but rather an intimate walk alongside Christ their creator. Greg Ogden notes,

---

[9] Wilkins, 93.

"Disciples are made in 'iron sharpens iron' intentional relationships."[10] and adds,

> All of these programs can contribute to discipleship development, but they miss the central ingredient in discipleship. Each disciple is a unique individual who grows at a rate peculiar to him or her. Unless disciples receive personal attention so that their particular growth needs are addressed in a way that calls them to die to self and live fully to Christ, a disciple will not be made.[11]

Ogden brings a crucial point; it is about the uniqueness of the individual that is of interest to Jesus and not acquiring knowledge. Ogden writes, "Information alone does not lead to transformation. We can hold truth in a compartmentalized fashion without having it change the way we think, feel or act. We can subscribe to a set of beliefs without allowing them to affect our lifestyle."[12] Jesus' core aim is not to transfer knowledge to the disciples, but on the contrary, walk with them through the complexity and obscurity of life, and help them learn how to navigate the drudgery and pain of life through the imitation and replication of His life. For that reason, Christ takes

---

[10] Greg Ogden, *Transforming Discipleship: Making Disciples a Few at a Time* (Downers Grove: InterVarsity Press, 2003), 43.

[11] Ogden, 43.

[12] Ibid., 44.

upon himself the responsibility in calling disciples to follow him.

David Platt in his book, *Follow Me*, points out, "When Jesus came on the scene in human history and began calling followers to himself, he did not say, 'Follow certain rules. Observe specific regulations. Perform ritual duties. Pursue a particular path.' Instead, he said, 'Follow *me*.'"[13] Platt brings an essential point of the 'call' in Jesus' methodology for doing discipleship. Not only does Jesus call disciples to follow him, different from the Pharisees whose students must ask to be their followers, but also His concept of "follow me" denotes something deeper than what the disciples know from their surrounding culture. For that reason, we need to examine in depth the meaning behind Christ's call to "follow me". What is the significance of these two words? Moreover, what does it entail, is it a requirement as a believer? In answering some of these crucial questions, we will be able to understand Jesus' intentions in asking us to follow him.

---

[13] David Platt, *Follow Me: A Call to Die. A Call to Live* (Carol Stream: Tyndale House Publishers, 2013), 54.

Understanding the Call of Jesus: Follow Me!

To understand Jesus' words "follow me", one needs to go back to the gospels, particularly the gospel according to Matthew 4:18-22, Mark 1:16-20 and Luke 5:1-11. After Satan's temptations on the mountain, Jesus begins his ministry in Galilee. He goes to the Sea of Galilee where he finds a couple of fishermen and calls them to follow him. The Gospel of Matthew states that, "As he walked by the Sea of Galilee, he saw two brothers, Simon, who is called Peter, and Andrew his brother, casting a net into the sea—for they were fishermen. And he said to them, "Follow me, and I will make you fish for people." (Matthew 4:18-19.) In the Greek, the word "follow" is not one word, rather the writers of the three gospels refer to two words: δεῦτε (come; follow) and ὀπίσω (after; behind; back). The Greek-English Lexicon Louw-Nida of the New Testament renders the word δεῦτε, as an adverb denoting an "extension toward a goal at or near the speaker and implying movement—'here, hither, come here."[14] It is also good to note that according to Strong's dictionary it is an imperative form of the word ĕimi (to go); come hither!:—come, follow[15]. Furthermore, to understand the actual meaning of Jesus' call to the disciples, we need to examine in depth the word ὀπίσω. Louw-Nida lexicon denotes it as a "marker of one who is followed as a leader (occurring with a variety of verbs indicating change of state or movement)—'after, to follow'."[16] Moreover, The Theological Dictionary of the New Testament states that, "As an adverb it means "from behind" in Mk. 5:27 (Mt. 9:20; Lk. 8:44) and "behind" in Rev. 4:6; 5:1. As a preposition it means "behind."[17] It also states,

> In the NT ὀπίσω is generally of theological significance when combined with the genitive of person or a verb of motion. In all the other expressions in which ὀπίσω occurs with a genitive

[14] Johannes P. Louw, and Eugene Nida, *Greek-English lexicon of the New Testament: based on semantic domains* (New York: United Bible Societies, 1996), electronic ed. of the 2nd edition., Vol. 1, p. 722.

[15] Strong, J. *A Concise Dictionary of the Words in the Greek Testament and The Hebrew Bible* (Bellingham, WA: Logos Bible Software, 2009), Vol. 1, p. 21.

[16] Johannes P. Louw, and Eugene Nida, *Greek-English lexicon of the New Testament: based on semantic domains* (New York: United Bible Societies, 1996), electronic ed. of the 2nd edition., Vol. 1, p. 469.

[17] Gerhard Kittel, Gerhard Friedrich, and Geoffrey W. Bromiley, *Theological Dictionary of the New Testament* (Grand Rapids, MI: W.B. Eerdmans, 1985), 702.

of person or verb of movement a very close relation is expressed between the persons in question. In the Synoptists it is usually Jesus who, by the call: δεῦτε ὀπίσω μου (Mk. 1:17; Mt. 4:19), summons the disciples to follow Him and binds them to Himself.[18]

When Jesus commands the disciples to "follow", he summons them to "come behind" him to unite their lives with his, to bring their lives together in a relational aspect. To come behind Jesus is a journey of entire dependence on him. Platt writes,

> With these two simple words, Jesus made clear that his primary purpose was not to instruct his disciples in a prescribed religion; his primary purpose was to invite his disciples into a personal relationship. We are not called to simply believe certain points or observe certain practices, but ultimately to cling to the person of Christ as life itself.[19]

Jesus' way of discipleship is not like the Jewish disciples of his day. The purpose of discipleship is not to go through a certain program and graduate

---

[18] Seesemann, H. (1964–). ὀπίσω, ὄπισθεν. G. Kittel, G. W. Bromiley, & G. Friedrich (Eds.), *Theological dictionary of the New Testament* (Grand Rapids, MI: Eerdmans, 1964), electronic ed., Vol. 5, pp. 290–291.
[19] Platt, 54.

from it after couple of weeks or months. However, the command to "come after me" is a way of doing life, directing the totality of the person toward Christ and his kingdom. Wilkins observes that,

> Discipleship was not simply a program through which Jesus ran the disciples. Discipleship was life. That life began in relationship with the Master and moved into all areas of life. Discipleship was not just development of the religious or spiritual dimensions, discipleship was directed toward the whole person.

Wilkins describes that Jesus' main purpose in having followers is to bind them to his purpose and the call of the kingdom. Christ calls the disciples to himself to change them from the inside out in order to have a relationship with him as he has with the Father. The disciples grow to become like Christ.

In attempting to apply Jesus' model in the church, one needs to ask the question if Jesus' call to follow him is physical or figurative. Wilkins makes a distinction that the Twelve had a unique calling to follow Christ physically in establishing the kingdom. At the same time, throughout Jesus' ministry he calls people to follow him in a figurative way. He writes, "While following Jesus around physically was intended only for the Twelve and for some of the broader group of disciples, figurative following was required for all."[20] Jesus says to the crowd, "Whoever does not carry the cross and follow me cannot be my disciple" (Lk 14:27). In this passage, Jesus reminds his hearers that to follow him one needs to die to self but not carry the cross in a literal and physical sense. He says it in a figurative way. Wilkens comments,

> Jesus did not expect the crowds to go find a literal cross. The figurative cross stood for dying to their own will and taking up the will of the Father as found in discipleship to Jesus. "Following Jesus" is to be understood in a figurative sense as well, meaning for the crowds to put their decision into action by committing their ways to Jesus' way. Even though they could not follow Jesus physically, were to follow him in the figurative sense of putting into action their faith commitment to him.[21]

The call to follow Christ is a serious matter and not to be lightly taken. To follow Christ is to cleave to him and his kingdom. Stuart Briscoe in his book, *Everyday Discipleship for Ordinary People* brings the marriage illustration of "leaving" and "cleaving" to describe the cost of discipleship. He writes, "When

---

[20] Wilkins, 131.
[21] Ibid., 131.

Jesus talked about marriage He insisted that there should be a "leaving" and a "cleaving" if marriage was to be successful. It was exactly the same for the disciples. If they were going to *cleave* to Jesus Christ, they would have to be willing to *leave for* him."[22] Jesus is in need of disciples who leave and cleave to his mission statement, choosing to imitate him in every area of their lives. According to Briscoe,

> As far as Jesus' original followers were concerned, their specific ministry necessitated that they be away from home for periods of time and that they could no longer make their living by fishing. For them, following Christ included a challenge to decide if what *He* wanted them to do rated ahead of what *they* wanted to do with their homes, families, and businesses. Or to put it another way: were they prepared to acknowledge His lordship of their lives in general with particular references to these specific areas?[23]

Briscoe paints a picture of how Jesus' disciples understood the call to "follow him" back in the first century. Therefore, what does it mean to leave

---

[22] Stuart Briscoe, *Everyday Discipleship for Ordinary People* (USA: Scripture Press, 1988), 29.
[23] Ibid., 31.

everything and what does it look like for modern disciples, especially for Gen Z and the coming generations? One needs to remember, from observing examples from the OT and the NT, and from looking at the original language, that Christ's call to follow him is a biblical command that is for every believer without exception. Yet, it is a choice that every follower of Christ needs to make. According to Bonheoffer discipleship is God's grace to us.[24]

---

[24] Clifford, 471.

Summary

In this more thorough understanding of the historical, biblical, and theological background of the call to discipleship, it is good to remember that Jesus' call to follow him is a biblical mandate. It is also crucial to note that following Christ denotes a sense of leaving and cleaving, denial of self, and being in a personal relationship under his lordship. Jesus calls every generation to die to self, pick up their cross albeit figuratively and to follow him. Although the technique is different from one generation to another, the call to follow behind the Master is the same for all believers. We must δεῦτε ὀπίσω μου – Jesus is calling us to bind ourselves to Him.

PART 3

The Discipleship Project: iDisciple (project DGZ)

Introduction

12-year-old Dre Parker finds himself a stranger in China due to his mother's career move. He feels lonely and discouraged that he does not have a chance against Cheng, the school bully, and his kung fu skills. Dre's fighting skills are no match for Cheng, but he finds a friend in his apartment's maintenance guy Mr. Han, who teaches him kung fu to beat Cheng in the next tournament. Now you know what movie I am taking about. It is The Karate Kid by Will Smith. I love this movie for it highlights the relational aspect of mentoring between Mr. Han and Dre.

In the beginning of Dre's training, Mr. Han tells him to drop and then pick up his jacket and hang it on the wooden hanger he made for him in his backyard. This is due to the incident that happened in his apartment between Dre and his mother asking him to hang his jacket on the hanger rather than throwing it on the floor after coming back from school. Dre's behavior is similar to Gen Z's lack of patience in this instant gratification society. Dre does not want to make an effort to hang his jacket just as Gen Zers are dependent on technology to do everything for them, rather than taking the time to do it themselves. They want things to be done fast and be done now, rather than wait. The Karate Kid is a great example of what Generation Z needs to see in a mentor. This generation needs someone to believe in them and needs someone like Mr. Han to take them outside of their social media bubble and toward an outside goal for the good of their community.

In this section I will talk about this rising generation: Generation Z. Next, I will look at the characteristics of mentors and their roles in discipleship. Lastly, I will address in depth the steps and processes a mentor needs to take in implementing the Navigator's 2:7 series discipleship curriculum in a relational atmosphere specifically targeting Gen Zers.

Understanding Gen Z

Every generation has a different understanding about the coming generation's politics, society, values, behaviors, and religious worldviews. For example, the Baby Boomers, born between 1946 and 1964 are known for their cultural and economic changes.[25] The following generation, Generation X, born between 1965 and 1979, are known for their entrepreneurial spirit, concern for quality of life, and for appreciating diversity.[26] Millennials or Gen Y are born between 1980 and 1994 and are the generation that experienced the emergence of technology and the internet.[27]

During this time, Generation Z, born between 1995 and 2012, comes on society's radar, especially when it comes to marketing. Gen Z is a high-tech generation. It is what David Bryfman refer to as the "iGeneration"

---

[25] Nicole Guerrero Trevino, "The Arrival of Generation Z on College Campuses" (PhD diss., University of the Incarnate Word, 2018), 31-36, PROQUESTMS.

[26] Ibid., 31-36.

[27] Ibid., 31-36.

and the "Selfie Generation."[28] According to Nicole G. Trevino, "They are experts at multitasking and tend to spend their free time communicating online and texting on their cell phones."[29] Nonetheless, they are a diverse generation and are accepting of other racial demographics. Trevino writes, "Since this generation has grown up with anti-discrimination and pro-family legislation all around them, they are expected to be more diverse and accepting of others."[30] Gen Z is open to many different worldviews because they are a part of an environment that places importance toward social justice, education, and technology.

---

[28] David Bryfman, "Teens Don't Need Our Praise, They Need a Place at the Table," *Baltimore Jewish Times*, Baltimore Vol. 361, Iss. 3 (March 2018): 9, 11.

[29] Trevino, 36.

[30] Trevino, 36.

Traits and Characteristics

Gen Z is a generation that is born in a time where social media is at its highest. Trevino points out that this generation has grown up surrounded by technology and social media, creating a generation that is smart and in-tune with the world around them.[31] They are the generation of video games, Facebook, Instagram, and Snapchat. Gen Zers can multitask across different platforms at the same time which include television, phones, laptops, desktops, and tablets.[32] In her book, *iGen*, Jean M. Twenge claims "iGen is spending much more time online and texting and much less time with more traditional media such as magazines, books, and TV."[33] This reminds me of the time my older neighbor saw me carrying a couple of books and expressed to me that only few people in our younger society today carry books due to phones, laptops, and tablets. Technology runs through their veins; it is in

---

[31] Ibid., 37.

[32] Ibid., 37.

[33] Jean M. Twenge, *iGen: Why Today's Super-Connected Kids Are Growing Up Less Rebellious, More Tolerant, Less Happy – and Completely Unprepared for Adulthood* (New York: ATRIA BOOKS, 2017), 68.

their genetic DNA disposition. Twenge states, "iGen high school seniors spent an average of 2¼ hours a day texting on their cell phones, about 2 hours a day on the internet, 1½ hours a day on electronic gaming, and about a half hour on video chat. That totals to six hours a day with new media."[34] Electronics and media are part of Gen Z's everyday life. This is the only thing they know because it is what they were born into; a world of instant gratification and fast-paced answers. Any other way of socializing becomes difficult because they do not have the ability to endure struggling as their Gen X and Gen Y predecessors.[35] According to Bencsik Andrea, Horváth-Csikós Gabriella, and Juhász Tímea, "A virtual world is natural for Y and Z, but a lot of them cannot fit their online life into their offline life."[36] For this reason, the Z generation is always struggling to fight between two identities: one that is virtual and the other that is actual.

Nevertheless, Gen Zers are more impatient than their former generations, more active, and looking for new challenges and desires constantly. At the same time, due to internet resources they are not afraid of continuous changes in their society for they use the internet to solve problems that come in their way.[37] Trevino states, "Due to their online presence, they

[34] Ibid., 51.
[35] Andrea Bencsik, Gabriella Horváth-Csikós, and Tímea Juhász, "Y and Z Generations at Workplaces." *Journal of Competitiveness* 8, no. 3 (September 2016): 93-94.
[36] Ibid., 93-94.
[37] Ibid., 93-94.

have a tendency to communicate in symbols using emojis. They are also concerned about privacy and prefer to remain anonymous as they engage online."[38] Trevino brings to our attention the loneliness of this generation. Even though they need recognition, the world and society they surround themselves with push them to live between two identities: the cybernetic, computer-generated and the physical, tangible self.

Due to the gap between the virtual and actual identities, Gen Zers are more prone to psychological, emotional and mental diagnoses in their fast-everyday life. They are more prone to anxiety, disappointment, and waiting for somebody to recognize and to give them positive feedback as their predecessors did with their parents by telling them that they are fantastic.[39] It is not surprising that loneliness and depression are on the rise among this generation. Twenge argues that even though this generation is always on their phones and social media, it does not exclude the fact that they are lonely. She observes, "A stunning 31% more 8th and 10th graders felt lonely in 2015 than in 2011, along with 22% more 12 graders. This is a monumental change in just four years. Teens are now lonelier than at any time since the survey began in 1991."[40] The rise of loneliness brings with it a rise in depressive disorder leading to self-harm and suicide. Twenge reveals how, "Teen's depressive symptoms have skyrocketed in a

---

[38] Trevino, 37.
[39] Ibid., 93.
[40] Twenge, 97.

very short period of time. The number of teens who agreed 'I feel like I can't do anything right' reached all-time highs in recent years, zooming upward after 2011."[41] Loneliness and depression are two behaviors that characterize Gen Zers, making them more inclined toward suicidal thoughts and acting upon them. It is the impact of social media on iGen'ers that gives rise to supplying and sharing a part of their lives rather than sharing a wholistic view; giving others a false view of a well lived life that has mostly successes.

---

[41] Ibid., 100.

Learning Technique

Gen Z learning methods, motivation and skills are different than Millennials, Gen X, and Baby Boomers. This generation is all about technology and fast information more than its former generations. High school, colleges, universities, and churches need to embrace new changes and techniques when it comes to learning and teaching curriculums on campuses, schools and Sunday school classes. Curriculums need to reflect the individual learning style that corresponds with the emerging iGen'ers.[42] Researchers claim that having different ways to learn by giving students the platform to work individualy, with others in small groups, and interacting with professors and their classmates are ways to engage Gen Z'ers.[43]

Nonetheless, professors, teachers, pastors and volunteers need to use more technology and media in the classroom to be able to engage this generation and grab their attention. Twenge states, "iGen'ers need textbooks that include interactive activities

---

[42] Trevino, 45.
[43] Ibid., 46.

such as video sharing and questionnaires, but they also need books that are shorter in length and more conversational in their writing style."[44] To bring the best out of this generation, professors and teachers need to use ultramodern technology styles to bring about participation in the classroom. Bobbi Shatto and Kelly Erwin report, "Methods such as flipped classrooms and active learning allow students active participation (e.g., case studies, group projects, use of clickers for voting, blogs, and critical thinking assignments.)."[45] The use of media such as YouTube videos is one way to catch Gen Z's attention and bring about participation between their peers. Trevino reveals, "Many of them have reported using videos as a classroom tool and 33% of them report watching lesson online."[46] Videos, online lessons, and eBooks are the number one learning techniques that this generation aligns with because it is the only methods they understand.

Nevertheless, the attention span for this generation plummets negatively verses earlier generations. Researcher Joshua Conran reports, "The attention span for this generation has gone down by 4 seconds in the last 14 years. In 2000, children were said to have a 12 seconds attention span while today, they have an 8 seconds attention span."[47] Also, Taylor,

[44] Twenge, 65.
[45] Bobbi Shatto, PhD,R.N., C.N.L. and Kelly Erwin M.A, "Teaching Millennials and Generation Z: Bridging the Generational Divide," *Creative Nursing* 23, no. 1 (2017): 25.
[46] Ibid., 46.
[47] Trevino, 45.

Doherty, Parker and Krishnamurthy conclude, "That generation Z students learn by observations and practice, not by reading and listening to PowerPoint presentations and that the average generation Z individual has an eight-second attention span, down from 12 seconds for Millennials (generation Y)."[48] The above statistics suggest that to win Gen Z'ers over and raise a successful generation, teachers of any institute, college, university, and church, must change their learning techniques, and be able to adapt to the forthcoming generation's way of communication and learning styles.

---

[48] Ludmila Mládková, "Learning Habits of Generation Z Students," Kidmore End: Academic Conferences International Limited, (2017): 699.

The Role of Church leaders in Discipleship

After understanding the makeup of Gen Z, from their traits, characteristics, and learning practices, it is crucial to look at the role of the pastor as a teacher and a guide for this generation through the execution of making disciples. The role of pastors, especially youth pastors and volunteers, are crucial in bringing up the next generation in the fear of the Lord. In his book, *Meet Generation Z,* James Emery white writes, "In our world, increasing numbers of people lead their lives without any sense of needing to look to a higher power, to something outside of themselves. Leaders of science and commerce, education, and politics – regardless of their personal views – do not tend to operate with any reference to a transcendent truth, much less a God."[49] The pastor and the pastoral leadership are key to discipleship because they know the "Biblical" worldview than any other teachers. White points out

---

[49] James E. White, *Meet Generation Z: Understanding and Reaching The New Post-Christian World* (Grand Rapids: BakerBooks, 2017), 7.

that many people such as coaches, good friends, and professors in both secular and non-secular universities and colleges can be mentors, but what distinguishes pastors is that God commissions them to teach His truth to His people, the church. They are the voice of absolute truth in a world that is contrary to it. He adds, "The heart of secularism is a *functional* atheism. Rather than rejecting the idea of God, our culture simply ignores him."[50] Gen Z is a generation living in a world that pushes God away, making them think that God is an option rather than the only way, the truth and the life. It is for this reason, the church, especially pastors and teachers of the word of God are key in denouncing these heretic beliefs in a world going further away from the "Biblical" truth of Jesus Christ. The only people who have a voice during these times are the pastors who shepherd the church, for this is their call from their Heavenly Father.

To understand how to teach this technical generation, we need to review the idea of discipleship. According to Matthew, Donald Hanger defines a disciple as a "pupil" or "learner."[51] He says, "The act of discipleship occurs as a disciple is being nurtured in the teaching of his/her master... the act of discipleship is the process by which disciples are trained."[52] To raise up the next generation

---

[50] Ibid., 8.

[51] John H. Aukerman, *Discipleship That Transforms: An Introduction to Christian Education from Wesleyan Holiness Perspective* (Anderson: Francis Asbury Press, 2011), 258.

[52] Ibid., 258.

of disciples, pastors and the pastoral leadership need to change their traditions in teaching about discipleship, and embrace newer methods that goes alongside this future generation - Generation Z.

The pastor's role in discipleship is a relational role between his/her disciples. It is this relational aspect between mentors and mentees that makes disciples willing to trust and carve time in their busy schedule to grow alongside their teacher and peers. Leon M. Blanchette writes, "The best way to develop a new generation of disciples who understand what it means to be followers of Christ is for the church to understand its role in the disciple-making process." To disciple the coming generation, the church needs to understand the learning practices and the societal and genetic roots every generation grows up with to have an effective discipleship relationship that transforms believers from followers to disciples for the kingdom of Christ.

The Art of Disciple-making

There is an art to everything in life. The art of communication, the art of conflict resolution, the art of interviewing, the art of money management, and time management, etc. Disciple-making is an art the church needs to acquire in turning followers into disciples for the kingdom of God. Jesus paints a great picture of disciple-making during his life with his disciples that the church needs to adopt to be effective disciple- makers as the Master. The question for church leaders is what are these unique steps? In his book, *Following the Master,* Michael J. Wilkens identifies five stages of what he calls "The Jesus Movement." These stages replicate the art behind what it takes to be a disciple of Jesus during his earthly ministry.[53] The stages according to Wilkens:

Stage One: Personal Initiative to Follow Jesus

The characteristic of the first stage is people taking the initiative to follow Christ. People that shepherd the

---

[53] Wilkins, 101.

church need to understand that everyone comes to the church with various personal initiatives to follow Christ. In the time of Jesus some came thinking He was the Messiah, His teaching and miraculous signs attracted others, people saw Jesus as a prophet, and others followed because their families and friends told them about the miracle worker.[54]

Stage Two: Jesus' Call

This stage in Jesus' ministry begins when he starts preaching that the kingdom of God is near. It is during this time that Jesus' call separates true disciples from regular followers. Only those who responds to the call are true disciples. Jesus is the only one who initiates the call. Jesus calls the believers to a higher calling; a denial of self and into an intimate relationship with the creator. It is fundamental for all ministry leaders to explain the dynamic of the call to discipleship to the congregation, for after people understand they have the choice to obey or refuse. I believe people do not know because they lack information. As the Bible states in Hosea 4:6a, "My people are destroyed for lack of knowledge." Without the correct knowledge of discipleship believers will be Christians but never disciples. Nonetheless, it is Jesus gracious call to the church; it is the gift of God to be part of and coworkers of His kingdom.

---

[54] Wilkins, 104.

Stage Three: Jesus Sifts the Followers

Jesus gives the invitation to the crowd and they follow, but at this stage he filters his followers. The writer of Hebrews 11:6 writes, "And without faith it is impossible to please God, for whoever would approach him must believe that he exists and that he rewards those who seek him." Faith is the only way to satisfy the one who calls. At the same time, as Bonhoeffer acknowledges, "There is no path to faith than obedience to Jesus' call." It is a two-sided coin; one side is faith and the other is obedience. It is the church's responsibility to teach that without both, followers cannot be disciples for Christ, for faith and obedience are the pillars of biblical discipleship.

Stage Four: The Limited Group of Followers

In proclaiming the Gospel, Jesus' followers decrease to only a few. Those few are the next generation of disciple makers who go proclaiming the gospel to all the nations after learning from their true Master. As good servants, pastors of any ministry are to follow in the steps of Jesus in working with the few, for those are the ones who will die to self, take their up cross and follow wherever the commands of God lead. them in the world. In looking at Jesus' example, we see He only chose twelve people to closely disciple, giving the church an example to follow. It is also helpful to remember that it is not in our own strength that we make disciples. In the book of Judges, God tells Gideon to sift through his worries by giving them a test. After the testing of the Lord, only 300 out of 22,000 soldiers remains to go to war with the Midianites. This small number was to display the power of God.

Stage Five: The Early Church

Through making disciples out of the few the early church is built. The Great Commission is the central method for building and growing the church. Wilkens emphasizes, "The Jesus movement of the first century continued as disciples made other disciples and then helped them to grow in faith until the time when they would enter into the glorified kingdom of God. Of such is what all true Jesus movements are made."[55] It is this concept of multiplication that the church needs to embrace in its focal mission statement. Every leader that has an influence on the few is to pass the baton to the next generation. Generation X and Y are to pass the torch of discipleship and disciple making to iGen'ers to build a generation ready to lead the coming generation in the knowledge of Christ. It is like the domino effect where once it starts it keeps going with more momentum than the beginning. That is how church leadership needs to think every time they disciple believers who say "Yes" to the gracious

---

[55] Wilkins, 119.

call of Jesus in becoming a disciple. The momentum keeps increasing until God stops it when He calls the church home.

These five general stages are applicable to all generations, including Gen Z, and important in understanding leader's approach in mentoring their congregations. It gives mentors a basic guideline to follow Christ's model in establishing the right relationship between mentors and mentees. Jesus' method is the foundation of discipleship, but the methods of implementation will be different from one generation to another.

Implementation of the Navigator's Methodology for Gen Z

In this section I will layout the processes of doing discipleship for Gen Z using the tool of Navigator's 2:7 curriculum series. Furthermore, I will look at my own research to examine Gen Z's mindset, from my own church, and how to help church leaders overcome those obstacles; especially the issue of time and trust.

Step One: Biblical Education

First, I recommend that pastors and youth pastors take the initiative to teach about the idea of discipleship to the church on a couple of Sundays. In my questionnaire to high school students and young adults in my own church, many lacked the true "Biblical" understanding of what it means to be a disciple. The result of teaching about it will cause discipleship to move from just official church leaders to all mature believers in the church. In this way church leaders are not the only people discipling others, but the whole body of Christ is walking in Jesus' steps, answering the call to making disciples. Jim Putman and Bobby Harrington writes, "In the educational category, a church uses the bulk of its energy on biblical education, and it's understood that the pastor's job (along with the pastoral staff) is to provide this education for the people."[56] This is a very important step before starting any curriculum about discipleship. Youth pastors should prepare a sermon series on the topic of discipleship and answer the following questions: "Is it biblical?" and "Is it mandatory?" for the growth of believers in the church. According to my questionnaire, all 55 high school students I interviewed claimed that discipleship is important for the person who follows Christ, but only 38 students (69%) claimed that having a mentor is optional, while 17 students (31%) claimed that it is not optional. These statistics reveal the misunderstanding of Gen Z's view on discipleship and its importance on their lives. If all 55 claimed that discipleship is important but only 31% stated that it is not optional, it shows the lack of biblical education for Gen Z'ers. This displays the confusion this generation is living with when it comes to the topic of discipleship and its importance in their lives.

---

[56] Putman, 25.

Step Two: Time

Out of my own curiosity, every Gen Zer I encounter in different churches and my own ministry, I take the initiative to ask them their views in regard to the ideas and issues of having and not having a mentor, and being in some sort of a discipleship relationship. The number one issue that I always hear is the issue of time. Time is the biggest hindrance to the topic of discipleship when it comes to having a mentoring relationship with Gen Z, and when it comes to the church pastoral leadership. Pastors and leaders in the church have taken their focus away from discipleship and into program making and how to grow the church. White writes, "Churches are too concerned with money and power, too involved in politics and too focused on rules."[57] Programs are good, but when it takes the true focus away from the true vision of disciple making, then the church has lost the true focus of Christ, which is making disciples. In her capstone thesis, Juliana Ford writes,

> How busy are we? If we do not have time for this, I wonder what we sacrifice at the idols of busy and productivity? For some, perhaps there are legitimate reasons - some seasons of life can be more demanding than others. But for many others, I would challenge them to

---

[57] White, 46.

look at their schedules and see where they can find one extra hour in their month.[58]

Juliana brings to her reader the importance of making time and makes us perceive the consequence of not making time to disciple and meet with this new generation that is in need of direction and guidance in their lives. I bring my voice with Juliana and I wonder what are we sacrificing for lack of time? I wonder if we are sacrificing too much. Juliana adds, "If we do not have time for this, not just in this season - but ever, where are we spending our time? And are we idolizing the counterfeit god of Busy? Mentoring is Kingdom work. It matters, and it matters that we make time for it."[59] Mentoring is Kingdom work, and I would also add that it is the way pastors walk in Jesus' steps when He chose his disciples. It is the stage where pastors and volunteers open themselves to believers to follow Christ through their actions and true biblical characteristics. Jesus gave time to His disciples, to come behind him, observing His ways of tackling the toughest and roughest situations of life that they encountered together during His ministry on earth, by establishing an example for them to follow. In having margins in the pastors' lives, they will be

---

[58] Juliana Ford, "The Magic of Mentoring: Vital Strategies For Recruiting Mentors For Undergraduate Students" (Capstone Project., Azusa Pacific University, 2019), 37.
[59] Ibid., 33.

able to dedicate their time to what is true and what grows the kingdom, which is the church.

One of The Navigators' rules, before starting one-on-one discipleship or mentoring a group, is the great emphasis on commitment from both the mentor and the mentee's side. If there is no time to commit to meeting together, then there will not be an effective discipleship. Pastors and leaders need to not merely talk the talk but also walk the walk. Gen Zers need to see authenticity in the person they share their lives with. In the above-mentioned movie, The Karate Kid, Mr. Han devotes his time teaching Dre true kung fu and that he needs to use it only for good and not for evil. At the same time, he is always there in his house, after his daily job, waiting for Dre to start his training. I believe pastors need to work according to their pupils' time frame, like the example of Mr. Han, to lead them to success in becoming disciples of Jesus, training them to become apprentices who make disciples for the advancement of the Kingdom.

Step Three: Trust

Another factor that hinders this growing generation, Gen Z, in entering a mentoring relationship is the matter of trust. In my own research and talking with many Gen Zers in my church, trust ranks the highest in terms of not being in a mentor and mentee relationship, compared to the aspect of time due to a negative experience in the past. To have an authentic and open trust between mentors and mentees, church leaders need to use different ways in bringing believers into a trusted relationship and to be able to give new hope for those with a negative experience.

Steps for Building Trust:

Invite others for group gatherings – To help ease believers in the discipleship process it is crucial that the church have couple of events where new believers, and those with past negative experience, feel that they are part of a group, making new friendships with their peers and their leaders. Open group gatherings gives mentors the ability to be free to get to know mentees in a non-structure form, giving mentees the liberty and the independence to be themselves, engaging in conversations that is not solely targeted toward their faith and beliefs, rather a platform to get to know other people that share the same values and ethics.

Develop relationships – the many group gathering will develop relationships between peers and leaders. It is through these developed relationships over several gatherings that discipleship gets build subtly without mentees knowing that they are on the way of developing and entering a meaningful relationship called discipleship. Leaders can ask deeper questions to assess Gen Z's maturity when it comes to biblical understanding. Moreover, during the open gatherings they will be able to see the positives and weaknesses of their characters and be able to call them into a relational aspect of discipleship at the right time. To engage this high-tech generation, leaders can use the social media platform to engage with their students throughout the week, reminding them of meetings, new events and gatherings, and asking them to be a part of the organization committee, letting them feel that they belong, focusing on a bigger goal outside of their social media bubble. This will strongly build and develop the relationships between each other and the leaders. Furthermore, it will build trust for those who are new believers and will affirm trust for those with bad experiences.

Follow behind me – Jesus took the disciples alongside his life journey as did Paul with Timothy. He also chose the few according to the above Wilkens steps of Jesus' methodology with the disciples. In this stage of building trust, the pastor and pastoral staff are able to ask Gen Zers to come alongside them as they run errands for the church or their homes, visiting the sick, buying food for the homeless, and even teaching them to share their faith with other people such as their families and friends. This can be in a group setting or individually. According to my questionnaire, when Gen Zers in my church where asked which layout preference for discipleship they preferred, 76% favored three people in a group, 20% chose one-on-one, and 4% leaned toward both, stating that all depends on where the individual is in their discipleship process. Jesus' model of *follow behind me* shapes the mentor and mentee's relationship where mentors can speak into mentees lives to correct, encourage, and even giving constructive advice. This will help Gen Zers to feel appreciated from their previous generations and be able to open to their leaders and come to them for different life advices when they are in need without feeling rejected. Gen Z will be able to trust their leaders as they observe the actions and behaviors of their leaders during different situations. As my mentor used to tell me, "People don't care about what you say, they care about what you do." Gen Z wants to trust leaders who talk the talk but also walk the walk. It is through these steps pastors and pastoral staff can build trust between leaders and Gen Zers.

Step Four: Implementation of the Navigators methodology for Gen Z

After going through the above process of achieving time and trust with Gen Zers, leaders will be in a good place to call believers into taking a more structured and deeper aspect of discipleship; which is studying the word of God together along their peers to have a meaningful life rooted in a biblical worldview.

There are many different discipleship programs out in the market, but with any curriculum leaders need to pay attention to how Gen Z pick up and store information. As we saw above, this generation has a very short attention span and like to engage with some form of technology to grab their attention. For this project, I chose the Navigators' discipleship program called 2:7 series. It is a three-book curriculum that takes the disciple from the beginning of the faith until sharing, witnessing, and discipling others for Christ. For this book I am using the methodology of this series and not the actual material. As a reminder, for any discipleship to succeed, establishing the commitment among the group is crucial. Per Jesus' example, according to Wilkens' steps above, I suggest that leaders choose three in a group, not exceeding twelve. This strategy will give disciples a more intimate and relational aspect between peers and leaders.

The Navigators' methods for Gen Z

Step One: The Commitment

As I said earlier, commitment is crucial to the success of discipleship. Gen Zers need to feel independent, at the same time, responsible. In the opening meeting, leaders need to create a video that explain the process of what will be taking place during their meeting times together. In that way, Gen Z will know up front what to expect from what they are signing up for. Next, establish the exact time and how often you will meet. According to the Navigators, groups need to meet once a week to be able to be effective, no more than two weeks. For my generation, Gen Y (Millennials), meetings used to be for one hour, but for Gen Z, due to their attention span, I would suggest meeting for no less than forty-five minutes as an adequate time in covering the material.

Step Two: The Setting

The setting can be flexible depending on where everyone lives. Groups does not have to meet at the church every week. I suggest in establishing a rotating schedule that meets at different houses or different coffee places. To be able to engage Gen Zer's technological mind set, leaders can start an account on different group messaging apps to remind and communicate with the group during the week. In this way, everyone gets all the notifications of any changes that might arise in the schedule.

Step Three: The Material
(According to the Navigators Methodology)

Everyone will have their bibles and notebooks to write and take notes. According to the Navigators' method, there must be a verse memorization for every session. The verse will be part of the reading lesson that is a part of a biblical story. Leaders can choose either to study the Old Testament or the New Testament, but for first time believers I would start studying the book of John and move to the rest of the gospels, finishing with revelation then starting the Old Testament. For each chapter, leaders need to prepare questions relating and tying it back to the studied story, engaging the group in conversations, and ending with a practical aspect that Gen Z can go out with and be able to implement during the week.

Additionally, during the week, leaders need to remind the group of memorizing the verse using the group messaging app by writing it down while they memorize it. Also, at the following meeting, Youth Pastors are to start each session with pairing people together, telling them to recite to each other the memory verse. In this manner, Gen Z will be able to learn and engage with their peers, forming a deeper relationship, showing them that they are not alone in this discipleship journey. After this section, leaders need to ask if there are any questions, concerns or input from last week's lesson. After answering all concerns and questions, leaders need to start the next lesson with a new memory verse.

In presenting this material, leaders should ask for the group's participation in reading aloud the chapter of the day while using PowerPoint presentations to keep them focused. Lastly, leaders are to use the group messaging app to do life with their group in asking them about their daily lives, and if any are in need of prayers when encountering tough situations in their lives etc. This will make Gen Z understands that they are not the only ones struggling with an issue, or are alone in life, rather it will show them that their peers' healthy filled lives are also full of failures and successes. In this manner, the church will help Gen Z go out of their loneliness and depressed state, stopping any attempts of suicide.

In summary, applying all the four methods above, will orient both mentor and mentee back to what true and biblical discipleship looks like, giving mentors the tools for how to disciple and discipline their mentees; at the same time, mentees will know up front what they are in for, giving both of them a platform to live life together peacefully.

Final Thoughts

I could not see myself without the aspect of discipleship. Every time I look at this rising generation my heart aches to see great young men and women living life alone without mentors to come alongside them to encourage, uplift, and bring out the God hidden gifts that are inside each one. I am thankful for my mentor, pastor Adham, who believed in me. I am the person I am today because of he took the time to disciple me according to the biblical worldview and trusted me to do the same for the next generations as long as I am breathing. This capstone project taught me things about Gen Z that I will take to heart and instruct other leaders and pastors in the church to come together and build upon this project to have a comprehensive, wholistic, and relational aspect of making disciples. I am grateful for Jesus calling me to follow behind him and extending the grace and gift of discipleship. I will extend the same grace to Gen Z and to the next generations to come.

Bibliography

Aukerman, John H. *Discipleship That Transforms: an Introduction to Christian Education from a Wesleyan Holiness Perspective.* Anderson, IN: Francis Asbury Press, 2011.

Barth, Karl. *The Call to Discipleship.* Minneapolis, MN: Fortress Press, 2003.

Bencsik, Andrea, Gabriella Horváth-Csikós, and Tímea Juhász. 2016. "Y and Z Generations at Workplaces." *Journal of Competitiveness* 8, no. 3, http://0-search.proquest.com.patris.apu.edu/docview/182 6360588?accountid=8459.

Briscoe, D. Stuart. *Everyday Discipleship for Ordinary People.* USA: STL Books, 1988.

Bryfman, David. 2018. "Teens Don't Need Our Praise, They Need a Place at the Table." *Baltimore Jewish Times*, Mar 16, 9-9,11. http://0-search.proquest.com.patris.apu.edu/docview/202 0723152?accountid=8459.

Ford, Juliana, "The Magic of Mentoring: Vital Strategies For Recruiting Mentors For Undergraduate Students". Capstone Project., Azusa Pacific University, 2019.

Green, Clifford J, and Michael P DeJonge. *The Bonhoeffer Reader.* Minneapolis, MN: Fortress Press, 2013.

Hull, Bill. *The Complete Book of Discipleship*. Colorado Springs, CO: NavPress, 2006.

Kittel, Gerhard, Gerhard Friedrich, and Geoffrey W. Bromiley, *Theological Dictionary of the New Testament*. Grand Rapids, MI: W.B. Eerdmans, 1985

Louw, Johannes P. and Eugene Nida, *Greek-English lexicon of the New Testament: based on semantic domains* (New York: United Bible Societies, 1996), electronic ed. of the 2nd edition., Vol. 1.

Mládková, Ludmila. 2017. *Learning Habits of Generation Z Students*. Kidmore End: Academic Conferences International Limited. http://0-search.proquest.com.patris.apu.edu/docview/1967 756545?accountid=8459.

Neudecker, Reinhard. 1999. "Master-Disciple/Disciple-Master Relationship in Rabbinic Judaism and in the Gospels." *Gregorianum* 80 (2): 245–61. https://search.ebscohost.com/login. aspx?direct=true&AuthType=sso&db=lsdar&AN=ATLA00 00988930&site=ehost-live&scope=site.

Ogden, Greg. *Transforming Discipleship: Making Disciples a Few at a Time*. Downers Grove, IL: InterVarsity Press, 2003.

Pentecost, J. Dwight. *Design for Discipleship: Discovering God's Blueprint for the Christian Life*. Grand Rapids, MI: Kregel Publications, 1996.

Platt, David *Follow Me: A Call to Die. A Call to Live*. Carol Stream: Tyndale House Publishers, 2013.

Putman, Jim, Bobby Harrington, and Robert E. Coleman. *DiscipleShift*. Grand Rapids, MI: Zondervan, 2013.

Shatto, Bobbi, PhD,R.N., C.N.L. and Kelly Erwin M.A. 2017. "Teaching Millennials and Generation Z: Bridging the Generational Divide."

Creative nursing 23, no. 1: 24-28, http://0search.proquest.com. patris.apu.edu/docview/1878391087?accountid=8459.

Strong, J. *A Concise Dictionary of the Words in the Greek Testament and The Hebrew Bible.* Bellingham, WA: Logos Bible Software, 2009, Vol. 1.

Trevino, Nicole Guerrero. 2018. "The Arrival of Generation Z on College Campuses." Order No. 10808667, University of the Incarnate Word, http://0-search.proquest.com.patris.apu.edu/docview/2055240184?accountid=8459. ProQuest Dissertations & Theses Global.

Twenge, Jean M. *iGen: Why Today's Super-Connected Kids Are Growing Up Less Rebellious, More Tolerant, Less Happy – and Completely Unprepared for Adulthood.* New York: ATRIA BOOKS, 2017.

White, James E., *Meet Generation Z: Understanding and Reaching The New Post-Christian World.* Grand Rapids: BakerBooks, 2017

Wilkins, Michael J., *Following the Master: A Biblical Theology of Discipleship.* Grand Rapids: Zondervan Publishing, 1992.

Printed in the United States
By Bookmasters